Moat House

1543
7·006

1542
3·162

1576
1·238

1575
·818

1577
2·021

1579
4·711

1578
·968

1580
·695

1605

SUTTON COLDFIELD

1606
1·845

1610
3·033

1611
5·170

Sewage Tank

1607
1·427

Sutton Town Station
(Midland)

1609
1·459

Three Tuns Hotel

P.O.

Fire Engine Station

Infant School

Town Hall

Holy Trinity Church

Grave Yard

Smithy

Sand Pit

Dog Inn

1608 ·409

1661
1·008

Signal Post

1662
1·132

1669
1·055

1670
14·312

167
·25

1660
·938

1663
1·103

1668
·260

1667 3·694

Slash Lane

1659
2·340

Signal Post

1664
·835

1672

1658
1·297

1665
·931

1666
4·230

Gas Works

1657
1·339

1655
6·657

1654
·575

King's Arms Inn

B.M.361·5

1673
5·623

356

1656
4·803

1697
·966

1696
·947

354

1706
2·590

1698
7·815

The Blabb

1699
·759

1705
2·445

1703
6·446

1702 1·903

1701
1·465

1741

1704
2·335

Holland House

1700
·250

1740

Signal Post

1742

SUTTON COLDFIELD
A Pictorial History

Shops in the Parade, *c.*1910.

SUTTON COLDFIELD
A Pictorial History

Sue Bates

Phillimore

1997

Published by
PHILLIMORE & CO. LTD.
Shopwyke Manor Barn, Chichester, West Sussex

ISBN 1 86077 037 1

Printed and bound in Great Britain by
BIDDLES LTD.
Guildford, Surrey

For Rebecca and Jennifer—
the future of Sutton belongs to you

List of Illustrations

Frontispiece: The Parade, *c.*1900

Illustration Acknowledgements

Birmingham Faces and Places (1889), 38, 160; Dugdale (*Antiquities of Warwickshire*, 1656/1754), 3, 129; Mrs. M. Evans, 22-3, 29, 38, 62, 70; Ted Hicken, 48, 154, 173-4; Noel Hird, 15, 36, 49, 50, 109, 122, 157, 166; *Illustrated London News*, 112; Midgeley (*Short History of the Town and Chase of Sutton Coldfield*, 1904), 2, 6, 19, 46, 47, 121; Jean Powrie, 16-40; Mrs. P. Price, 35; Ian Privett, 169-71; St Peter's Church, 108; W. Smith, 5, 126, 153; Mrs. L. Stonehouse, 75; *Sutton Guide Book*, 17, 30, 34; Sutton Coldfield United Reformed Church, 51-3, 76-7, 163, 176; Mike Tuddenham, 58, 71-3; Warwick County Record Office, 4, 8-12, 25, 28, 45, 56, 111, 124-5, 130, 142; Miss Warwood, 114-20; Roy White, 21, 29, 41, 64, 80, 82, 87, 96, 141; Sue Bates, 13-16, 18-20, 22, 26, 27, 31-4, 37, 39, 40, 42-4, 54, 55, 57, 59-61, 63, 65-9, 74, 77-9, 81, 83-6, 88-95, 97-107, 110, 113, 116, 122, 123, 126-8, 131-5, 143-52, 155, 156, 158, 159, 161, 162, 164, 165, 167, 168, 172, 176;

Acknowledgements

I would like to record my thanks to those who have helped me to research and prepare this book. In particular my thanks go to: Chas Hammond, Mr. Bridgewater, Rev. R.F. Jenkins, Terry Jones, Mrs. Mary May, Mr. J. Perks, Holy Trinity Church, and Mr. A.W.T Hemming for information; to Mrs. Jean Powrie, Mrs. Pat Price, Mrs. Janice Moore, Mrs. May Evans, Miss Warwood, Robin Jones and Mr. Roy White for information and help with photographs; to Ian Privett, Mike Tuddenham, Ted Hicken, Noel Hird, Mrs. Lily Stonehouse, June Lawrence, Warwick Record Office, Sutton United Reformed Church and St Peter's Church, Maney for use of photographs. Thanks also go to John Bates for help with research, to Rachaell Docker for typing the index and to Noel Hird for his help and support; and lastly to Tabitha who constantly proves that four paws are better than two fingers for typing. While every attempt has been made it was not always possible to trace copyright holders of some photographs. Any opinions, conclusions and mistakes are mine alone!

Introduction

Until 1974 Sutton Coldfield was situated in the extreme north west of Warwickshire at the boundary with Staffordshire. The settlement grew up on a long, narrow ridge consisting of Lower Keuper sandstone, above the place where a road leading to Lichfield forded the Ebrook stream. The road passed through the hamlets of Maney, Little Sutton and Hill in addition to Sutton itself. The area to the east is principally composed of Keuper Marl covered by superficial boulder clay and gravel. To the west Hopwas Breccia and deposits of Bunter Pebble beds result in the open moorland of Sutton Park. The soil in the area was poor, although more land was used for agriculture by the 19th century.

The name Sutton means 'south town', and there has been some debate about the identity of its northern partner. William Dugdale, in his *Antiquities of Warwickshire*, 1656, stated his opinion that Sutton was 'south' of Lichfield, which could link in with neighbouring Middleton (the 'middle town'). Others, including members of the William Salt Archaeological Society, have considered that the settlement was 'south' of Cannock Chase. The Coldfield (or 'col-field') was a large area of heathland situated to the west of the town, which may have been used by charcoal burners. Much of the Coldfield was situated in Staffordshire. Francis Smith described it in *Warwickshire Delineated*, published around 1819, as 'much overgrown with gorse and presenting a very bleak and barren appearance'.

Shakespeare (who had relations from his mother's family living at Peddimore Hall) mentions Sutton in *Henry IV* when Falstaff says 'Get thee before to Coventry, fill me a bottle of sack, our soldiers shall march through: we'll to Sutton Coldfield tonight.'

A large expanse of woodland was contained within the boundaries of the manor. The combined woodland and heathland adjoined Cannock Chase and formed part of the royal hunting chase belonging to the kings of the Saxon kingdom of Mercia. It is likely that Sutton developed as a hunting lodge.

Recent field walking by members of the Birmingham and Warwickshire Archaeological Society (BWAS) has revealed evidence indicating the presence of hunter-gatherers in the area in the mesolithic period (6000-4000 BC).

The Roman Rycknield Street runs in a north/south direction about two miles to the west of the town, crossing Sutton Park on its way to join Watling Street. Archaeological evidence found by BWAS suggests possible Roman settlements to the east of Sutton around Hermitage Farm, Ox Leys Farm and Grounds Farm.

By the time of King Edward the Confessor the manor of Sutton was held by Edwin, Earl of Mercia. Domesday Book of 1086 recorded that Earl Edwin 'held' (in the past tense) the manor. It was noted that the woodland was two leagues wide and one league long. It is probable that the manor had already reverted to the crown after the execution of Edwin following an unsuccessful uprising in 1071.

There is evidence of cultivation in the Middle Ages, especially in the eastern part of the parish, which suggests that woodland had been cleared for agriculture (a procedure known as assarting). Remains of ridge and furrow have been found near Peddimore Hall. There were several moated sites in the area, remnants of which still occasionally survive (for example at Peddimore Hall and Pool Hall).

In the 12th century Henry I exchanged the manor with lands held by Roger, Earl of Warwick, and the Chase (which was a royal preserve) became a Park where the Earls hunted. Guy de Beauchamp, Earl of Warwick, was granted a charter in 1300 permitting a market on Tuesdays and an annual fair on the eve and feast of the Holy Trinity (a movable feastday) and the two days following. This market may have lapsed, as a further charter in 1353 permitted a market on Tuesdays and annual fairs on the eve, feast and morrow of the Holy Trinity and the eve and feast of St Martin (in November). For a time the town prospered but reverted to the king once more following the fall of the Earl of Warwick in 1478 during the Wars of the Roses. The town then fell into decline, the market was abandoned and, according to William Smith writing in 1829, the town 'was quickly proceeding to a state of ruin and desertion'.

A remarkable change occurred in 1528 when Henry VIII granted a charter to the town which gave self government to the inhabitants and granted them the town, manor and park. Government was in the hands of the Warden and Society—a fellowship or corporation of 24 residents chosen for life and selected from the most prominent inhabitants. The King was persuaded to grant this charter by John Harman, or Vesey, who was born in Sutton around 1465. Vesey held several offices in the Church, most notably serving as Bishop of Exeter 1519-51. He was also favoured at Court by Henry VII and Henry VIII and held various state appointments including that of tutor to Princess (later Queen) Mary, daughter of Henry VIII and Katharine of Aragon. The charter also entitled Sutton to be styled the 'Royal Town'.

Bishop Vesey was generous to his native town and made various improvements at his own expense, including the erection of a Moot (or Town) Hall. He built houses for the poor, founded a grammar school, paved the town, and attempted to curb the robberies on the main highway.

Crime on the roads near Sutton was a problem for centuries. Highway robbery, and sometimes murder, occurred, especially on the routes passing to the west of the town. A famous incident happened in 1324 on a road known as the Ridgway (which probably followed the course of the old Roman road through Sutton Park) when Elias le Collier was robbed of £300. The felons were not caught and Elias sued the authorities in both Warwickshire and Staffordshire (because the road formed the boundary between the two counties). Although the court found in his favour poor Elias seems to have received little compensation from the sheriff of either county.

During the Civil War in the 17th century Sutton seems to have favoured the Parliamentary side and there were several prominent Roundhead families in the area such as the Pudseys at Langley Hall. Tradition states that Oliver Cromwell visited the town in August 1643 and Prince Rupert's troops passed through in the same year.

From time to time complaints arose over the administration by the corporation and another charter was granted by Charles II in 1664 'for the improvement of the town and the amendment of evils'.

In the 17th and 18th centuries Sutton became a commercial centre, and many water mills were created as a source of power. Trades included making bayonets, axes, forks, knives, buttons, barrels for guns and cotton spinning. John Wyatt was a local resident who produced an invention to aid this last process. 'Great numbers' of people were employed. Most of the mills were situated in or near Sutton Park and reservoirs were formed to provide the water required for the mills.

Two turnpike roads were created in the 18th century, one now known as the Chester Road, which followed a route to the west of Sutton Park and replaced the earlier route across the Park, and another passing through the town to Lichfield. Highway robbery continued to be a problem and many highwaymen are reported in the greater Sutton area, including the legendary Dick Turpin.

It was during the 18th century that Sutton received the first migrants from Birmingham when some of the newly prosperous manufacturers moved out to the town and built new houses in the pleasant surroundings found there.

This trend increased dramatically after the arrival of the railway in the 19th century. The first railway station was opened in 1862 when the London & North Western Railway (LNWR) linked Birmingham and Sutton, with stations at Aston, Erdington, Gravelly Hill, Chester Road and Wylde Green. LNWR extended the line to Lichfield in 1884. Peers' *History and Guide of Sutton Coldfield*, published in 1869, described Sutton Station as 'a neat, commodious building, and the servants seem models of civility'.

A second railway line opened in 1872 when the Midland Railway created a route from Wolverhampton to Birmingham which arrived at Sutton by crossing Sutton Park. This route caused a great deal of controversy with accusations made that the Park was damaged by allowing 'a great scar' to be made. Stations were opened at Streetly, Sutton Park, Sutton Town and Penns. The line was closed to passenger traffic in 1965 and now carries freight only.

Sutton Station was the scene of a disastrous rail crash on Sunday, 23 January 1955 when an express running from York to Bristol (which had been diverted because of engineering works) was derailed, killing 17 people. The train had taken the bend approaching the station at twice the 30 m.p.h. speed limit.

The arrival of the railway resulted in rapid increases in population as more families moved out of Birmingham to live in the fresher, cleaner air of Sutton. In 1801 the population numbered 2,847 which had increased to 4,574 in 1851. This figure increased in the space of twenty years to 5,936 in 1871 and by 1901 was 14,261.

Commuters were not the only passengers to take advantage of the new method of transport to Sutton—the railway offered the opportunity for more people to visit the Park and excursionists were soon arriving in their thousands. Eyewitness accounts describe 'continuous streams' of visitors flowing in the direction of the Park, and this was to lead to a permanent change in the use of the Park. Some of the visitors were not at all welcome to the residents as there were reports of vandalism, rowdy and indecent behaviour. It became necessary to employ a policeman in an attempt to curb the unruly behaviour and an entrance fee was introduced to pay for this.

Most of the visitors to Sutton Park came to enjoy its natural beauty and respected the environment. The Park inspired many poetic efforts, including the following published in a pamphlet by Palmer & Holland at the Victoria Works, Aston, around 1873 and lent to the author by Mr. Roy White of Sutton Coldfield:

BEAUTIFUL SUTTON!

THE WILD AND THE FREE.

BEAUTIFUL Sutton! oh, dear unto me
　Are thy brakes and thy woodland, so open and free;
Thy dingles and dells, thy lakes and thy streams,
That flash in the light of the sun's golden beams;
So dearly and fondly I linger with thee,
Beautiful Sutton! the wild and the free.

Beautiful Sutton! swift-winged are the hours
I spend as I roam through thy deep-tangled bowers,
Thy beautiful swards and thy dark forest trees,
That gracefully bend to thy health-giving breeze;
Each season unfoldeth new graces in thee,
Beautiful Sutton! the wild and the free.

Beautiful Sutton! what may be the spell,
That all who have seen thee shall love thee so well?
It is nature, untrained and unconfined,
That strikes a chord in the human mind;
And feelings of melody blending with thee,
Beautiful Sutton! the wild and the free.

Beautiful Sutton! I roam at thy will,
Through the dark coppice, or down by the mill;
Thy cascades of water, so sparkling and clear,
Entrancing to see, and so charming to hear;
And music is heard from bush and from tree;
Beautiful Sutton! the wild and the free.

Beautiful Sutton! I gaze on thee now,
Thy vales in the shade, but the sun on thy brow;
The hues of the common are charming to sight,
Part lost in the gloom,—part bath'd in the light.
The daylight is waning, farewell unto thee,
Beautiful Sutton! the wild and the free.

The town's government remained in the hands of the Warden and Society until 1885, although by 1830 the corporation consisted of a warden, two justices and 10 aldermen. In 1885 the town became a Municipal Borough (under the terms of the Municipal Corporations Act 1882). The borough council consisted of a mayor, six aldermen, and 18 councillors. The town was divided into six wards : Trinity, Hill, Boldmere, Maney, Wylde Green and Walmley. Sutton was a member of the Aston Union of parishes for the provision of poor relief.

By 1908 the town was supplied with electricity (from works belonging to the Corporation), gas (from Birmingham Corporation Gasworks) and water (from South Staffordshire Water Works Co.).

Sutton had long enjoyed a reputation as a healthy place to live. Research work on 17th-century burial registers by members of the Sutton Coldfield Local History Research Group indicates that the inhabitants were fairly well nourished and healthy with a longer life expectancy than the average for the country at that time, and infant mortality was amongst the lowest in the country. The anonymous author of *The History of Sutton by an impartial hand*, 1762, observed that 'Sutton Coldfield is universally allowed to have a pleasant situation, an healthful air, its full proportion of all the accommodations of life, and an agreeable neighbourhood'. In his Annual Report for 1890 the Medical Officer of Health, Dr. Bostock Hill, reported that 'a sanitary condition has been obtained comparable with that of any health resort in the Kingdom'. In 1896 he could report that there had been no deaths in 1895 from smallpox, scarlet fever, diphtheria, typhoid fever or measles.

This reputation helped to attract many convalescent and nursing homes to the area. It also encouraged speculative builders to invest in the area, sometimes developing whole roads or estates at the same time. Several well respected architects (often from the Arts and Crafts Movement) worked on projects such as the Anchorage Road estate, which was developed around 1871.

Development has continued throughout the 20th century so that most of the Sutton Coldfield area is now occupied by housing and the ancillary requirements of shops, schools, churches and other public buildings. Some light industry is also present. The population recorded for Sutton in the 1991 census was over 90,000.

A major change in the history of the town occurred in the local government reorganisation of 1974 when the town became part of the Metropolitan District of Birmingham in the newly created county of the West Midlands. This change of status was viewed with mixed feelings by local residents.

The photographs which follow are intended to give an overview of Sutton's long and interesting history but inevitably space only permits a selection to be included. Those interested in the town's history are recommended to inspect the collections held in both Sutton and Birmingham Libraries. A variety of sources have yielded many photographs, some of which are published here for the first time.

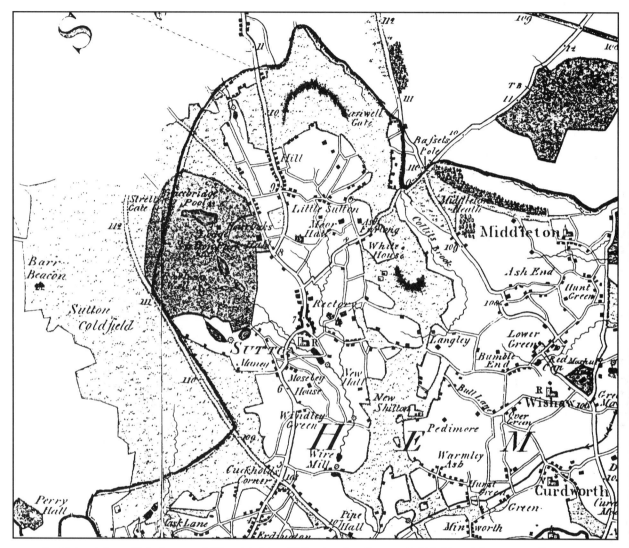

1　Extract from Yates' map of Warwickshire, 1789, showing Sutton Coldfield and its surrounding area.

Sutton Town

2 John Harman, alias Vesey, was probably born at Old Moor Hall, *c.*1465. After studying at Oxford he found favour with Henry VII and held various church appointments, most notably Bishop of Exeter from 1519. Vesey accompanied Henry VIII to the 'Field of the Cloth of Gold' in 1520.

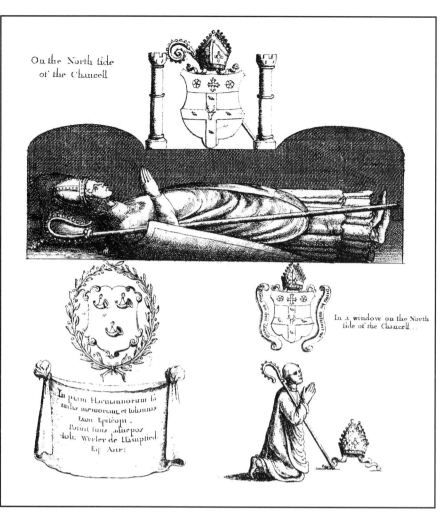

On the North side of the Chancell

In a window on the North side of the Chancell.

In primis Elemosinorum sit
miluc memoriam et Iohannus
Exon Episcopi .
Posuit huic aduc pos
Ioh: Wyrler de Langplied
Eq: Aur:

3 Vesey's handsome tomb in Sutton church is shown here in 1656, together with a picture of the bishop from a nearby window (which had gone by 1716).

4 Bishop Vesey became very wealthy and gave generously to Sutton (at the expense of Exeter). He built a moot hall and 51 houses, paved the town and rebuilt aisles in the church. He also procured the charter from Henry VIII in 1528. Vesey built a mansion for himself named Moor Hall (shown *c.*1720 when it had been extended), where he died in 1554. This house was demolished in the 19th century and replaced with the present house which is now a hotel.

5 A view of Sutton from the Park in 1829 showing the hill on which the town developed. In 1821 Sutton was 'a small market town, and large parish, situated in ... the county of Warwick ... in an excellent air' with principal trades of 'making barrels for guns, axes, knives, forks and buttons'. The population was 3,466.

6 High Street looking north, *c.*1850s. For centuries the High Street was considered to be the centre of the town and many fine buildings were erected here in the 18th century.

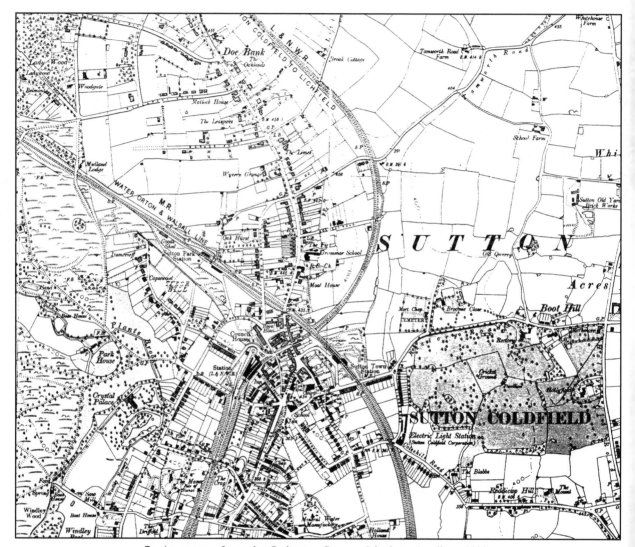

7 An extract from the Ordnance Survey 6 inch to 1 mile, *c.*1902.

8 High Street looking south towards the *Royal Oak Hotel* and the parish church, *c.*1904. Vesey House (shown right with bay windows) was the home of Miss Agnes Bracken, local historian and artist. The sculptor William Frederick Woodington was born in a nearby house in 1806. One of his most notable works is the relief on Nelson's column showing the Battle of the Nile.

9 The rear of Vesey House is shown here. Miss Bracken was the author of the first history of Sutton Coldfield, published in 1860. Vesey House has been converted for use as a shop and considerably altered.

10 A small weigh house known as the 'Pepper Pot' stood at the corner of Coleshill Street, Mill Street and High Street, adjacent to the *Royal Oak* (which was advertising a motor garage by 1907).

11 This view shows the 'Pepper Pot', with the *Royal Oak Hotel* and the *Old Sun*, Coleshill Street (both demolished *c.*1938 to make way for the Vesey Memorial Gardens).

12 Another view looking south along High Street to the *Royal Oak Hotel* in the early 1930s, before the Vesey Gardens were constructed.

13 A view of High Street looking north from the corner of Mill Street, *c*.1907, showing Midland Bank on the right and Vesey House on the left.

14 A postcard from around 1904 shows the Midland Bank and Lloyds Bank on the right.

15 The present *Three Tuns Hotel*, shown in 1997, dates from the 18th century but replaced a medieval building in which Oliver Cromwell is reputed to have stayed. The cellars from the earlier building have survived and are rumoured to be haunted by the ghost of a drummer boy killed in the Civil War.

16 The *Royal Hotel*, shown in 1997, was also built in the 18th century. Originally a private house, it became a hotel in the mid-19th century, known as the *Swan*. The name was changed in 1910 to avoid confusion with the older public house in Lichfield Road (known as the *Top Swan*).

17 Advertisements for two businesses in the High Street in 1907.

VESEY ME

18 *(left)* Several fine houses survive in Coleshill Street dating from the 17th and 18th centuries. Some of the buildings are attributed to the architect Sir William Wilson.

19 *(below left)* Church Hill from Mill Street looking towards the parish church, late 19th century. All the buildings on the left side of Church Hill, together with buildings at the corner of Mill Street and Coleshill Street, were demolished to make way for the Vesey Memorial Gardens.

20 *(below)* The Vesey Memorial Gardens were created in 1938 and include a large plaque recording the life and work of Bishop Vesey. The gardens are shown *c.*1938.

AL GARDENS, SUTTON COLDFIELD   H 1503

21 *(inset)*   Mill Street looking north, *c.*1914, with the Masonic Hall on the right. Designed by the architect G. Bidlake (father of W.H.) and built as the Town Hall in 1858/9 of red brick with stone facings, it was purchased in 1903 for use as the Masonic Hall.

22   Mill Street, *c.*1911. Mill Street took its name from a water mill formerly operating on the present site of the Lower Parade. The post office was located in Mill Street in the 1920s and '30s, when telegraph boys on bicycles could be seen delivering messages.

23 *(top left)* William Gibbins (shown here aged about 60) had a shop in Mill Street which he kept until his death in 1927. The shop sold antiques and had a cottage and stabling for a pony and trap behind.

24 *(bottom left)* William Gibbins' son Frederick had a greengrocer's shop in Mill Street. The quality of the produce was renowned. Mr. Gibbins junior also went into partnership with a local builder with whom he built many houses in the neighbourhood, including the development of the old rectory site. Mr. and Mrs. Frederick Gibbins are shown on their wedding day *c.*1919.

25 *(top right)* The Lower Parade looking towards the town's school (now the Baptist church) in the 1890s. The *Old Dog* (originally known as the *Talbot* and now called the *Knot*) is on the right.

26 *(bottom right)* The Parade, *c.*1900. In the Middle Ages a dam was constructed on the site of the Lower Parade forming a mill pool, which powered the water mill belonging to the Manor. A great flood broke the dam in 1668 and drained the pool. Although the mill was eventually demolished the road name continued as The Dam.

PARADE, SUTTON COLDFIELD.

27 The road known as The Dam was rebuilt in 1826 to improve the turnpike road. There were few buildings along its route until 1869 when a 94-year lease was granted on the land. Gradually new shops were built and a new name, The Parade (shown *c.*1912 looking north), began to appear by 1879.

28 The Parade looking north, *c.*1916, with an early motor bus. The area around the *Three Tuns* in the High Street was originally thought of as the town centre, but The Parade rapidly gained popularity and soon replaced the earlier focal point.

29 Henry Attkins & Son was listed as 'provision dealer' in *Kelly's Directory of Warwickshire,* 1908. By this time many tradesmen had opened businesses in The Parade including several grocers, drapers, druggists, boot makers and cycle dealers. There was also a fruiterer, a gasfitter, an ironmonger, a watch- and clockmaker and an undertaker.

30   E.R.J. Bayliss advertisement, *c.*1907.

31 *(below)*   The *Museum Inn* is shown on the right of this view of The Parade looking south, *c.*1907. The *Museum* was the first building constructed after the lease was granted in 1869.

32 Another south-facing view shows The Parade in the 1930s when traffic had become a problem. A one-way system was introduced with southbound traffic using the Lower Parade and northbound drivers using The Parade. The *Museum Inn* can be seen in the centre and Paris House (a dress shop) on the right.

33 Arthur Chamberlain's fruiterer's and greengrocer's shop was listed in *Kelly's Directory of Warwickshire*, 1940 at 109 The Parade. The shop also sold fish and poultry.

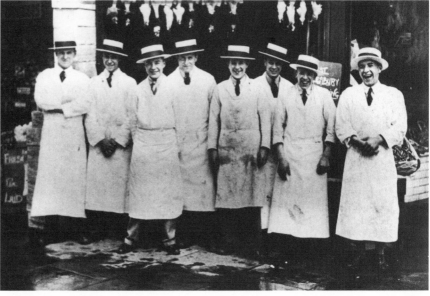

34 Arthur Edmund Horne's bakery was situated in Lower Queen Street and was listed in trade directories in the 1920s and 1930s. This undated photograph shows the bakery's horse-drawn delivery van. Many other tradesmen delivered to customers. William Bromwich's baker's shop was listed as being in the High Street in 1908.

35 Thomas Barratt opened the first radio shop in Sutton during the 1920s in The Parade and moved to the former gas showrooms in Mill Street in the 1930s. The building (photographed by Mr. Barratt's grandson in 1968) was demolished in 1969. Thomas Barratt died in 1969 and his son Eric carried on the business until 1977 at shops in Maney and New Oscott.

36 The first railway to Sutton opened in 1862 with a route from Birmingham through Aston, Erdington and Wylde Green. It was operated by London & North Western Railway and was a significant factor in the town's expansion, offering commuter transport from Birmingham. It also led to a change in the use of Sutton Park when excursionists had the opportunity to visit.

37 Council House from the south, *c.*1908. Situated near the railway station, this was designed by Edward Holmes and built by Mr. C. Jones (a Birmingham builder) as the *Royal Hotel* and opened in May 1865 hoping to take advantage of passengers arriving for holidays. It became a sanatorium in 1896 and was converted for use as the Council House in 1906.

Council House, Sutton Coldfield.

38 In 1886 (John) Benjamin Stone (shown *c.*1893) was elected first Mayor of Sutton Coldfield, an office he held until 1891. Born in 1838, he held various public offices in Birmingham and helped to revive the local Conservative party. He served as MP for East Birmingham, 1895-1900, and was a pioneer photographer, a writer and a traveller. He was knighted in 1892 and appointed first official coronation photographer in 1911. He died in 1914 and his photographic collection is deposited in Birmingham Reference Library.

39 Council House from the north showing the building with the 1906 extension designed by A.R. Mayston for use as the Town Hall. King Edward Square was named following the 1902 coronation, and the war memorial commemorated those killed in the First World War.

40 A production of *Cinderella* at Sutton Coldfield Town Hall.

41 When no longer in use the stocks were moved to a position in King Edward Square, under a thatched rustic roof erected for protection. The stocks were on wheels and the post at the side was the whipping post. The stocks were finally removed because of vandalism.

42 The two blocks of houses in Tudor Road were built between 1882 and 1914. Many similar houses were built in the town around the turn of the century to accommodate the rapidly growing population.

"HOME OF REST" SUTTON

43 Sutton was considered a healthy place and was the location of numerous nursing and convalescent homes. The 'Home of Rest' was founded in 1891 by Rev. H.F Kelvey in Clifton Road overlooking the Park. It offered rest, comfort and a change of air, diet, scene and society to working-class women and girls not well enough 'to follow their duties' but not ill enough to require hospitalisation. Contagious diseases and nursing cases were not admitted. Patients came from Birmingham, Walsall and the Black Country, often supported by charity. It was well used—for example, 281 patients were accepted in 1898.

Churches

The history of Christian worship in Sutton dates from at least Saxon times when a chapel was built by the Earls of Mercia at the Manor House on Manor Hill. The chapel was dedicated to St Blaise and was used for all services until the parish church was built in the 13th century. The chapel was finally demolished in the 15th century and there is a tradition that Bishop Vesey used some of the stone to create two bridges over the river Tame.

The population of Sutton increased rapidly in the second half of the 19th century following the opening of the railway. New churches, which eventually became separate parishes, were built in the more remote parts of the parish at Hill, Walmley, Boldmere, Maney and Whitehouse Common, followed in the 20th century by Four Oaks, Wylde Green and Banners Gate.

In 1772 the then rector recorded only three Roman Catholic families in the parish. The first post-Reformation Roman Catholic church was built in 1834 in Lichfield Road and more churches were created later in Boldmere, Walmley and Four Oaks.

Non-conformist activity was first recorded in 1672 when a house belonging to Samuel Stevenson was licensed for Presbyterian worship. Non-conformist worship was recorded again in 1772 when there was a meeting house for Independents which was also used by local Methodists. The first Congregational Church was built in Park Road in 1879-80. There are now United Reformed Churches (the successor to Congregational and Presbyterian Churches) at Sutton, Wylde Green and Banners Gate. The first Methodist church in Sutton was a Calvinist chapel built in The Parade in 1860. In 1937 the church moved to Queens Road, and the building became the town's first free public library. There is another Methodist church at Four Oaks. The first Baptist church in the area was built at the corner of Chester Road and Boldmere Road (a district known as 'Little Boldmere') in 1905 and was shortly followed by the Baptist church at the bottom of Trinity Hill in 1908. Churches followed at Four Oaks and Streetly.

Unfortunately space does not permit an illustration of every church building in the area. A small but hopefully representative selection follows.

44 The parish church (shown after 1898) was first recorded, dedicated to the 'Holy Trinitie', in a tax list of 1291 when it was valued at 20 marks.

45 The building was probably a simple nave and chancel. Many additions include the tower and north and south aisles (built around 1533) and a second north aisle added by the architect Yeoville Thomason in 1875-6.

46 The first rector was Gregory Harold, appointed in 1305. Seven members of the Riland family were rectors from 1689 to the 20th century (broken only by the incumbency of Richard Williamson 1843-50). John Riland is shown here, *c.*1790.

47 The church contains many monuments and memorials. A brass records Barbara, wife of Roger Eliot (rector 1595-1617), who died in 1606 aged only twenty-three. Her husband and children are also buried there. Another brass commemorates Josiah Bull who died in 1621 aged about fifty. Other monuments record local families such as Pudsey, Jesson, Sacheverell and Hartopp.

48 The tower was added by 1500 and used to appear to be taller because the pitch of the nave roof was made steeper in alterations following the collapse of the nave roof in 1759. Further alterations were made in the 19th century and the stained glass was designed for the east window by the firm of Gibbs in 1863. The architect C.E. Bateman decorated the chancel in 1914.

49 Tragic Mary Ashford was buried in the churchyard in 1817 after she was found drowned in Penns Lane, either by accident, murder or suicide. Circumstantial evidence pointed to Abraham Thornton who was found guilty by the Coroner's Court but was acquitted at Warwick Assizes. Mary's family then invoked an ancient statute to 'Appeal for Murder' countered by Thornton invoking 'Trial by Battel' (for the last time in England). Thornton eventually emigrated to the USA. Many of the tombstones and monuments in the churchyard have been removed, although some remain on the south side. The churchyard was enlarged in 1832 but by 1880 was almost full. A new cemetery was consecrated on 4 May 1880 in Rectory Road due to the efforts of the then rector, William K. Riland Bedford.

50 In 1995 a new church hall, named the Trinity Centre was opened, built on land formerly part of the graveyard. The new hall is a base for church events and also provides a meeting place for other social, educational and leisure-based groups.

51 In 1877 land was purchased in Park Road for £300 to build a Congregational church (shown 1917). The foundation stone was laid on 30 June 1879 and the opening service was held in April 1880. The building cost £2,628. In 1960 the spire was removed because it had become dangerous and in 1972 a new church centre was built adjacent to the church, which is now known as the United Reformed Church.

52 The chancel and vestries were added in 1890 and a Ladies' Parlour (now used as the church office) was built at the front of the church in 1902. The chancel was further altered in 1904 when a new stone pulpit was erected and the original gas lighting was replaced with electricity. The war memorial window was dedicated in September 1920 in memory of members killed during the First World War (a second plaque was added after 1945).

53 The first minister at the new Congregational Church was Rev. Joseph Shillito (left) who was appointed in 1884. Mr. Shillito retired in August 1896 and Rev. Frank W. Collyer (right) succeeded him in October 1896, remaining until March 1907 when he went to South Africa to take charge of the Central Church in Johannesburg.

54 The first Roman Catholic church opened in Lichfield Road in 1834 near the *Swan* public house and the grammar school. Dedicated to the Holy Trinity, the church could seat only 200 people and by the 1930s was too small for the increasing congregation. A new church was erected on the opposite side of the road and the original building (shown in 1997) became the 'Guildhall' and is now in commercial use.

55 The present Roman Catholic church, Lichfield Road.

Schools

56 Bishop Vesey founded the Grammar School in 1541. A famous 'old boy' is Richard Burton, author of *The Anatomy of Melancholy*, who was a scholar around 1586. The 'remains' of the original building, situated next to the churchyard off Trinity Hill, are shown here. The 'Sons of Rest' building now occupies the site.

57   The school moved to its present position in Lichfield Road in 1728. The building is shown in 1911.

58   The Grammar School building has been enlarged several times, notably in 1862, 1887 and 1906 when the new building was officially opened by Sir William Anson MP. This view dates from around 1960.

59 The cadets at Bishop Vesey Grammar School are shown in this Edwardian photograph.

60 This undated photograph shows a production (probably of *Iolanthe*) by the Bishop Vesey Grammar School Gilbert & Sullivan Society, which was still active around 1960.

61 A National School was first founded in 1825 at Sutton. This engraving shows the building on the corner of Mill Street and Trinity Hill following remodelling in 1870. It was enlarged again in 1888 and 1902. In 1825 another school was established near Hill and more followed at Green Lanes, Boldmere, Walmley, Maney and Roughly.

62 The Gothic-style building became too small and a second school was built on the opposite corner of Trinity Hill and Victoria Road in 1907 for use by the boys, while the girls remained in the older building. Some of the boys are shown here in 1935 at the celebration of the Silver Jubilee of King George V. Both schools are now used as the Baptist Church.

63 The Technical School was erected in Lichfield Road in 1903, near the site of the *Old Swan Inn* next to Bishop Vesey Grammar School (which can be seen in the background). It is now part of Sutton Coldfield College.

Events

64 Maypole dancing was revived in Sutton for the celebrations for Queen Victoria's Golden Jubilee in 1887. Later, Benjamin Stone presented an album to the Queen at Windsor Castle. Four of the girls were present but one was taken ill and was received separately by the Queen. This photograph is possibly from 1897.

65 An undated photograph by Royal Town Studio, Sutton Coldfield, shows an unknown procession, possibly at a carnival. The studio was in business in Maney by August 1914, run by A.W. and A.C. Aston. It last appears in *Kelly's Directory* for 1932.

66 Another photograph by Royal Town Studio shows a float decorated with 'GR'. George V acceded to the throne in 1910 and several major events followed including the Coronation 1911, Peace Day 1919, and the 'Sutton Pageant' in 1928 commemorating 400 years of Sutton's history. Empire Day was also celebrated every year and Sutton used to celebrate 'Trinity Monday' when there was a fair and procession.

67 Residents in fancy dress photographed by Royal Town Studio between *c.*1914-32.

68 Another Royal Town Studio photograph shows entertainments at a garden party *c.*1914.

69 A procession of little girls heading for the Park past a crowd of onlookers in July 1912.

70 During events in Sutton Park for the Silver Jubilee in 1935 of King George V and Queen Mary, schoolchildren made an enormous 'G' and 'M' (shown here). In 1937 children formed the flag of St George to mark the Coronation of George VI. Other events included a civic service, bell-ringing, a ball and a firework display. The mayor and mayoress, Councillor and Mrs. W.A. Perry, presented a new mace.

71 In 1957 Sutton Park was the venue for the ninth World Scout Jamboree. It was a jubilee event celebrating both the centenary of Lord Robert Baden-Powell's birth and the 50th anniversary of scouting. B-P created the word 'jamboree' to name the first international gathering of scouts at Olympia, London, in 1921.

72   The event lasted from 1-12 August and 25,000 scouts and their leaders from 84 countries attended, camping in the Park. There was a camp theatre, hospital, exhibitions and an arena where various displays were staged. A 'Gang Show' with two performances a night was held at the Birmingham Hippodrome, 5-10 August. The Duke of Gloucester opened the event and Olave, Lady Baden-Powell (B-P's widow) led the closing ceremony.

73   Queen Elizabeth II and Prince Philip visited the Jamboree on Saturday, 3 August. The Queen, Patron of the Boy Scouts Association, watched a March Past by representatives of all the nations present and there was a display by the Air Scouts.

Sport

74 An local football team photographed by Royal Town Studio before 1932. Sutton Town Football Club was formed in 1879 and their original ground was in Coles Lane.

75 Sutton Congregational Church Cricket Team. The photograph shows (back row): C. Cauthery, K.J. Woodcock, N. Dainty, G. Woodcock, N. Wood, C. Dainty. (centre): Rev. F.W.J. Merlin, A. Webb, J. Stephens, C. Burrow, W. Davis, H.W. Withers, R. King. (seated): C. Stonehouse, L. Jones, H. Degg (vice-captain), G. Parsons (captain), A. Wood, J.F. Woodcock (hon. sec), A.R. Waine. The boys at the front were H. Cauthery and S. Dainty.

76 The women's gymnasium class from Sutton Congregational Church in Park Lane, *c.*1911. The ladies gave an 'exceptionally good' display in April 1911 which included 'running the maze, free movements and Swedish marching'. Their teacher, Miss Powell, was praised for her enthusiasm and competence.

77 Skaters have used the frozen lakes in the Park for generations. These skaters were ignoring safety warnings in December 1961.

78 The Open Air Swimming Baths at Sutton Park (shown in 1924) were opened in 1887. Swimming used to be permitted in the early morning at Powell's Pool but it is now discouraged.

79 Sailing at Powell's Pool. The Sea Cadets train at Powell's Pool, and Sutton Sailing Club have their headquarters with an entrance in Monmouth Drive.

Sutton Park

81 *(right)* Town Gate (*c.*1913) is the nearest entrance to Sutton town, and is approached along Park Road—both were created following the 'Hartopp Exchange' of land in 1826. Wyndley Gate was formerly the nearest entrance to the town.

82 *(below right)* Tolls for non-residents of Sutton were introduced in the 19th century. This list dates from around 1881. In 1953 the admission charges were threepence an adult, one penny a child, one shilling a horse or motorcycle and two shillings a car. The parking fee for a motor coach was two shillings and sixpence. Entry to the Park has been free since 1974 when Birmingham City Council took over its management following local government reorganisation.

80 *(below)* Until 1826 Wyndley Gate was the nearest entrance to the town. Other entrances now exist at Boldmere Gate, Banners Gate, Royal Oak Gate, Streetly Gate, Four Oaks Gate, Blackroot Road and Town Gate. There are several additional pedestrian entrances.

HISTORY AND GUIDE
TO
SUTTON PARK,
BY
ABSALOM PEERS.

RULES & REGULATIONS.
CHARGES FOR ADMISSION.

On Mondays, Tuesdays. Wednesdays, Thursdays, and Saturdays, ... 1d.

On Fridays and Sundays,... ... ... 2d.

Children under seven, and Charity Schools, half-price.

For every Conveyance with one Horse ... 6d.

For every other Conveyance, per horse ... 6d.

For each Person on Horseback, ... 6d.

All strange Dogs found in the Park will be destroyed.

The sale of all articles in the Park is strictly prohibited.

No Fire to be lighted or Tents erected without special permission

Tickets of Admission to be produced to the Park Keepers on application, or the parties be re-charged.

All Persons committing any injury in the Park will be apprehended and prosecuted.

Bathing after nine in the morning is prohibited.

An Inspector and Body of Police will be employed to enforce the above Regulations.

PRICE ONE PENNY.

83 Meadow Platt (shown here in 1957) was created as a result of the 'Hartopp Exchange'. This popular area near Town Gate has provided a space for generations of children to play games.

THROUGH THE WOODS
IN SUTTON PARK

84 Sutton Park contains many remnants of the ancient woodland which once formed part of the larger forest. However, the woods have been subject to careful management for over a hundred years and are only partly natural. Many postcards survive from the early 20th century which were popular with the thousands of visitors arriving each year. This card was posted in 1910.

333. Gumslade, Sutton Park.

85 A postcard dated 1921 shows the path called Gumslade which leads through the woods in the north-east section of the Park. Ancient oaks survive along this route, and silver birch, rowan and holly are common, with alders and sallow near Bracebridge Pool. Several plantations of larch, Scots pine, spruce and beech have been created during the last hundred years. Although much woodland is today available as a public amenity some areas are kept for timber production.

86 Several springs rise in Sutton Park and flow into two streams—Plants Brook (sometimes called the Ebrook), shown here *c.*1920, and Longmoor Brook. The two streams merge at the eastern edge of the Park near Wyndley Leisure Centre and the joint stream joins the river Tame at Minworth.

87 All the pools in Sutton Park are artificial and Wyndley (shown here *c.*1910) is probably the oldest. It was part of a chain of pools until a great flood broke the dam in 1668. An ancient road crossed the Wyndley dam and joined the Driffold (or pound for animals pastured in the Park) with Sutton Manor House and went on to Coleshill. The pool once operated two watermills. It was absorbed into Sutton Park in 1937.

88 Keeper's Pool is named after John Holte, a keeper in the reign of Henry VI. Open-air swimming baths were opened here in 1887. The pool is shown in a postcard dated 1920.

89 A pretty 'Gothic' style cottage at Bracebridge Pool (shown *c.*1915) is reputed to have been used as a hunting lodge by Henry VIII. Partially rebuilt in the early 19th century it was a tea garden for many years and became a restaurant in the 1980s. Known as The Boathouse it has recently been the target of attacks by vandals but has now reopened.

BRACEBRIDGE COTTAGE
SUTTON PARK

90 Bracebridge Pool was made by Sir Ralph Bracebridge in the 15th century to supply bream to his household. Sir Ralph was given a lifelong lease by the Earl of Warwick in 1419 granting him the Manor House, park and pools in return for sending nine lancers and 17 bowmen to the garrison at Calais. The tea garden is shown here in the 1930s. Bracebridge Pool was purchased from the Hartopp family in 1869 by the Warden and Society for £1,520 with money gained by selling land to the North-Western Railway Company.

91 Freshwater fish were in great demand before the Reformation, especially by the wealthy. An Earl of Warwick is said to have paid more than fifteen shillings to have bream sent from Sutton to Yorkshire and baked in flour with spice, pepper, saffron, cloves and cinnamon. Fish remained popular and a pool was made for the rector's household in 1761 to stock carp—described by 1786 as 'great big creatures like sucking pigs'. This pike would have been at least 15 years old. Angling remains a popular sport in the Park, and a 30lb carp was caught in 1996.

92 Powell's is the largest pool and was created in the 18th century, probably by a member of the Gibbons family. It was incorporated in the Park in 1937. Boldmere Swimming Club used the pool for many years until 1907 when the 'Powell's Pool Company' increased the hire charge for use of the 'dressing sheds'. Swimming is no longer permitted in the pool, which was de-silted in 1938 to facilitate sailing. Sutton Sailing Club use the waters and have a clubhouse on Monmouth Drive. The Sea Scouts also use the pool and have a training ship there. In the Edwardian period a pleasure steamer called *Foam* was an attraction.

93 Blackroot Pool was created to supply water power in the 18th century. Its name derived from a large tree root formerly on an island in the pool, which was reduced in size when the Midland Railway line came through the Park in 1879. This Edwardian postcard shows visitors enjoying its attractions. Rowing boats could be hired from a boathouse.

BY LONGMORE POOL   SUTTON PARK

94 Water power was also the reason for the creation of Longmore Pool by John Gibbons, John Riland (Rector of Sutton) and William Rawlins in the 18th century. The mill (shown in an undated postcard) powered by the pool made buttons at first and was later used as a flour mill. The dam at Longmore Pool burst in July 1923 and the resulting flood caused much damage in the town.

95 Now a public house, Park House was originally the site of another mill. In the 18th century it was a blade mill and a tilt hammer was in operation here. It was purchased by Sutton Corporation in 1948 for £19,000. This view dates from around 1909.

96 In addition to woodland and water Sutton Park contains many acres of heathland, shown here near New Oscott in 1936. The heathland is very popular with visitors and supports gorse and heather together with other species. The heathland requires careful management to prevent the invasion of scrub and to ensure its continuation as open heath.

97 Many thousands of visitors have made use of the Park's various attractions. This photograph of Harry and Molly Carrington and their children David and Winnie shows a typical family outing in 1905.

98 Edwardian children are shown here at Wyndley Pool.

99 A group of factory girls are shown in this undated photograph enjoying a break in the Park.

Smethwick poor Children's FAF outing 1911.
We arrive at Sutton Park. No 7.

100 Sutton Park was the destination chosen for many group outings, especially those organised by charities. This outing was for the benefit of poor children from Smethwick in 1911. The children are shown arriving in a long column preceded by a band.

101 A second photograph shows the Smethwick children enjoying a picnic. Annual day outings were still being arranged for poor children from Birmingham in the 1920 and 1930s. Known as 'Ragged' or 'Royal Robins' they were often barefoot. They were brought on special trains in August. The town's traders helped with contributions–Mr. Gibbins sent apples and oranges from his greengocer's shop in Mill Street and there were free rides at Pat Collins Funfair. Sometimes the children were given boots, although it was rumoured that their parents sometimes sold them later.

Smethwick poor Children's FAF outing 1911

102 Entrepreneurs soon noticed the increased numbers of visitors when the railway opened. Mr. Job Cole from Perry Barr opened the Crystal Palace and Royal Promenade Gardens in 1868 on a 30-acre site between the Park and town. Mr. Pat Collins, a well-known local showman, acquired the lease in 1906 and operated a funfair with a 'Big Dipper' and other rides. The Crystal Palace was requisitioned in 1914 first as the headquarters of the Warwickshire Regiment 1st Birmingham City Battalion and later used for Commonwealth troops and convalescent soldiers. The funfair reopened in 1919. The lease on the site expired in 1962 and Sutton Town Council decided not to renew it. Wyndley Leisure Centre now occupies the site.

103 The first miniature railway was 10¼in. gauge and opened at the Crystal Palace Funfair in 1907. It was replaced by a 15in. gauge railway with a longer route which closed during the First World War. It operated briefly from 1922-4 and opened again in 1938; it was a popular attraction until 1962 when it was forced to close after the lease expired. Locomotive Number 1 (The Sutton Belle) is shown in 1955.

104 In wartime Sutton Park assumed different roles. In 1914 the Park was placed at the disposal of the Government. A training camp was set up for the 1st and 2nd Birmingham City Battalions of the Royal Warwickshire Regiment.

105 In the Second World War, camps were built for training the National Fire Service and to accommodate German Prisoners of War and internees (one of whom was the young Robert Maxwell). Later the American Army located their European Post Office here and American soldiers were billeted with local residents or housed in another camp. Trees were lost for timber and heathland was damaged by the camps, crop growing and tank testing.

106 The Park continues to attract visitors as it is an important amenity adjacent to a large conurbation. The Park hosts sporting events, and offers opportunities for walkers, cyclists, picnickers, joggers and others. Its varied habitats are environmentally important and it has an educational role. Some areas are closed to motor traffic. These crowds are shown on Whit Monday 1956.

107 Fire is a constant danger. These firemen were fighting a grass fire in the 1976 drought, when the Park had be closed temporarily after almost 450 acres were affected. Not all fires are accidental—the *Daily Mail* reported an arson attack in February 1903 which destroyed a thatched rustic arbor erected by Sir Benjamin Stone, mayor in 1889. An earlier fire in 1868 was also suspected arson. This was another drought year and the fire raged for several days, destroying more than 500 acres of gorse and trees. Described as a 'splendid spectacle' with a 'lurid glare' visible for miles, it was viewed by hundreds of people.

Maney

The name Maney was first recorded in 1285, and the name may mean a well-watered common (from Old English). The medieval Manor House of Sutton was situated on the hill at Maney still known as Manor Hill. The house was demolished by 1500. A chapel dedicated to St Blaize was situated at the Manor House and there is an ancient tradition that it was originally intended to build the parish church here but the stones were miraculously spirited away to the site on Trinity Hill. Several old houses survive at Maney, some of them built by Bishop Vesey. A famous resident was Dr. George Bodington who had a sanatorium at the White House (now the site of the Odeon Cinema). Dr. Bodington (who was also a local politician) published a famous paper on the treatment of tuberculosis in 1840 and also treated patients at an asylum for the mentally ill in Maney. Bodington Gardens next to the smithy commemorate him. Maney consisted chiefly of farmland for several centuries but in 1825 a road leading north from the Chester Road through Wylde Green to Sutton and Lichfield was turnpiked. In addition the arrival of the railway, with a station at Wylde Green, helped to attract newcomers and the population began to grow. In 1874 a National School was built in Duke Street, which was also licensed for use as a church by the Bishop of Worcester. By 1877 there was sufficient demand to found a district served by an 'iron church' erected at the expense of the Rector of Sutton, Rev. W.K.R. Riland Bedford. Another 'iron church' was erected by the Calvinists and a church hall made of corrugated iron was erected next to St Peter's Church in 1919.

108 St Peter's Church opened in 1905, replacing the 1877 'iron church'. The architects were Cossins, Peacock & Bewlay from Birmingham and the builders T. Elvins. A separate parish was designated in 1907 and Rev. Barry Drew was appointed first vicar.

109 It was 1935 before funds permitted building the tower to complete the original design of St Peter's, shown here in 1997 with the adjacent stone house.

110 The *Horse & Jockey* was originally a simple building but was rebuilt around the turn of the century. Situated at the corner of Jockey Road the names of the public house and the road derive from the horse racing activity in Sutton. The first racecourse was located near Blackroot Pool 1844-50, the second was at Westwood Coppice near Banners Gate 1868-79 and the third was at Four Oaks 1881-9. There was also a steeplechase course near Sutton Station *c.*1852-73. Two tragedies occurred at Banners Gate: in 1868 a horse ran into the crowd killing one spectator and injuring others, and 29-year-old Henry Taylor (principal trainer at Hednesford) was killed in 1870 when his horse fell.

111 The *Cup Inn* and the view towards Sutton.

112 The *Cup* also owes its name to horse racing. In 1846 a silver cup weighing 90 ounces was awarded to Jockey Frost riding 'Auld Squire' at the course started by Jack Wiggan two years earlier. The cup was presented by Mr. George Richmond Collis.

113 The *Cup* was rebuilt around 1900 and this postcard shows the new building and the view towards Sutton, *c.*1909.

Minworth and Walmley

The Manor of Minworth was recorded as 'Meneworde' in Domesday Book in 1086, held by Turchil of Warwick. The suffix 'worth' means a farm or property and the prefix is probably a personal name. It was probably merged with neighbouring Curdworth in the Middle Ages as both were usually held by the same person. Eventually Minworth became a detached hamlet of Curdworth until the northern and eastern half of the parish was transferred to Sutton Coldfield in 1931 following the Local Government Act of 1929. The remainder of the parish was divided between Birmingham and Castle Bromwich. The population of Minworth was 291 in 1801 and had only risen to 688 by 1901. In 1881 the Birmingham Tame and Rea Drainage Board constructed a sewage treatment plant at Minworth which now covers more than 700 acres.

Walmley was originally a hamlet of Sutton Coldfield. Its name probably derives from the Old English 'walm' meaning a bubbling up or swelling or boiling (meaning a strong spring). Walmley became a separate ecclesiastical parish in 1846. St John's Church was built in 12th-century style from blue bricks from a design by D.R. Hill and consecrated in 1845. The church has been replaced by a larger building and is now used as the church centre. Walmley School was built in 1826 at Signal Hayes. Walmley owes much of its development to the Webster family who constructed a forge mill at Penns in the late 18th century. Penns Hall, the Webster family home, is now a hotel.

114 Minworth Village Green (shown *c.*1923) was a common in the 18th century. An infants' school was opened in December 1900 to the side of the green, replacing temporary accommodation at a wheelwright's shop. A school for children aged 7-14 opened next door in 1902.

115 Minworth Congregational Church (shown *c.*1911) was situated near the canal. It was built in 1825 and was demolished in 1963. The Anglican Church of St George was consecrated in 1909 by the Bishop of Birmingham.

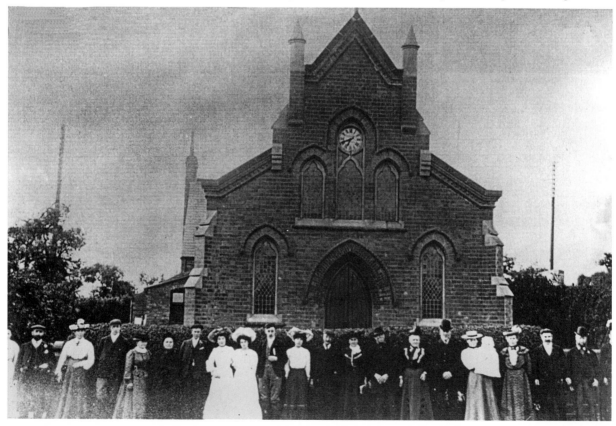

116 The Sunday School at Minworth Congregational Church, *c.*1900.

117 The Pittaway family lived at Minworth around 1900. Mr. and Mrs. Pittaway are seated with their daughter Edie (who died in 1985, aged 95). In the back row (left to right) are Floss, Sue, Jack, Liz and Nell.

118 Mr. and Mrs. Warwood are shown outside their cottage in Summer Lane, Minworth.

119 The wedding of Miss Edith Pittaway and Mr. Warwood on 27 August 1914. The couple are shown with their families and guests at Emily Cottage, Walmley Ash.

120 Ammunition workers at Frederick Mountford's factory in Minworth during the First World War. Back row (left to right): Eva Mansell, Edith Warwood (née Pittaway) supervisor, Marie Hunt, Mr. Smith, Rosie Walker and Beattie Caldicott. Front row: Alice Picken and Edith Mansell. The girls were making hand grenades which was potentially very dangerous work.

121 Peddimore Hall, situated to the east of Walmley, dates from around 1660 but replaced an earlier building. The hall (shown in the late 19th century) had an unusual double moat. The Arden family, who were related to Shakespeare's mother, lived here for many years.

122 Langley Hall (17th-century home of the Roundhead Pudsey family) was located 1½ miles north east of Walmley. This monument in Sutton Church commemorates Henry Pudsey (died 1677) and his wife Jane. Henry bequeathed Langley to his daughter Anne (wife of Sir William Jesson) and his remaining fortune to her sister Elizabeth (married to Lord Ffolliot). The memorial was made by the architect and stonemason William Wilson, pupil of Sir Christopher Wren, who became Jane's second husband. Denied permission to be buried in the family tomb, Sir William's grave is outside the church wall near his beloved Jane.

123 Forge Lane probably derived its name from the forge powered by Plants Brook, which provided water for several mills.

124 New Hall Mill, *c.*1900. The watermill was constructed around the end of the 16th century on Plants Brook. It survives as one of the last remnants of Sutton's industrial history.

125 New Hall Mill, *c.*1900. Plants Brook also powered wire drawing mills founded by the Webster family at Penns in the 18th century and Plants Forge Mill at Minworth, acquired by the Websters when they changed from production of iron to steel. Manufacture was transferred to Hay Mills around 1857. The business later traded as Horsfall & Webster.

126 New Hall (shown *c.*1830) is a moated house which was 'new' in the 14th century when it was built to replace a 12th-century house. It has been remodelled and enlarged several times, first in the 16th century by William Gibbons, brother-in-law of Bishop Vesey, and claims to be the oldest inhabited house in England.

127 Around 1586 the house was bought by Henry Sacheverell and enlarged again. The towers were added around 1796 and further alterations were made in the 19th century. New Hall became a hotel in 1985 and distinguished visitors include the Italian tenor, Luciano Pavarotti.

NEW HALL COLLEGE, SUTTON COLDFIELD.

PRINCIPAL - - - A. HASTINGS JONES (London University).

Late English Professor at the German Educational Institute, Antwerp; and formerly Assistant Master in the Mercers' Company's School, London.

ASSISTED BY AN EFFICIENT STAFF OF RESIDENT AND VISITING MASTERS.

EDUCATION.

The College is under entirely New Management, and has been thoroughly re-organised.

Pupils are prepared for either Professional or Commercial Careers. The results at the different Public Examinations have been eminently successful.

Particular importance is attached to French and German, a knowledge of which is so useful in Commercial Life.

SUCCESSES.

During the years 1898 and 1899 the following successes were obtained :—Four boys passed the Oxford Local Examinations; two boys passed the Chartered Accountants' Preliminary Examination; 18 boys passed the various College of Preceptors' Examinations; two boys obtained Pitman's Shorthand Certificates.

The 6th Wrangler (1899) was an old New Hallian.

OTHER PARTICULARS.

Delicate and Backward Boys receive special attention.

There is every accommodation for Boarders. The Bedrooms are large, lofty, well lighted, and thoroughly ventilated.

The place is remarkably healthy, and the health record of the School is unsurpassed, and during the past twelve months not a single case of illness has occurred.

The Diet is thoroughly wholesome and unlimited, and butter is procured from the private dairy.

There being over 20 acres of land attached to the College, ample opportunities exist for Football, Cricket, Tennis, &c.; while abundant facilities for Fishing are afforded by the moat and ponds.

There is a Carpenter's Shop, a well fitted Gymnasium, and a Chemical Laboratory.

Military Drill and Class Singing.

All further particulars may be obtained on application.

128 New Hall housed a boys' school from 1885 to 1903.

Little Sutton and Four Oaks

Shown as Four Oaks Hill on a map of 1725, there were few buildings in the area when Lord Ffolliot built Four Oaks Hall in the late 17th century. The railway arrived in 1884 when the London & North Western Railway extended the line from Sutton Coldfield to Lichfield. This prompted much development followed by a growth in population and the ensuing demand for churches, schools and shops. All Saints' parish church was consecrated in 1908 but it was only possible to build a nave and a temporary vestry at that time. Although a choir vestry was added in 1954 (following an attempt to finish the church as a War Memorial) it was not until 1965 that the building could be completed. Four Oaks Hall was owned by the Luttrell family in the 18th century. Anne Luttrell (whose father became the Earl of Carhampton) married first a Derbyshire squire called Horton but, being widowed, married Henry, Duke of Cumberland in 1771. This so annoyed the Duke's elder brother, George III, that he refused to receive the new Duchess, and it resulted in the Royal Marriage Act which forbids members of the royal family to marry without permission from the Crown.

The present building called Moor Hall was built by the Ansell family (of Ansells Brewery) in the 19th century and is now a hotel. A golf course also takes its name from the house.

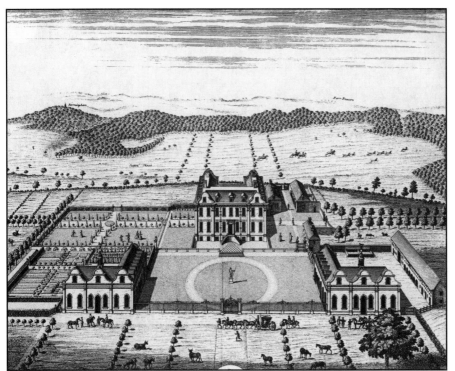

129 Four Oaks Hall and its park, *c.*1719. Built by Henry, 3rd Lord Ffolliot, around 1680, it is usually attributed to the architect William Wilson who was Lady Ffolliot's stepfather. The land had been part of Sutton Park but the Charter granted by Henry VIII allowed enclosure of 60 acres to construct a dwelling.

130 Sold to the Luttrell family in 1744, it was eventually purchased by Sir Edmund Hartopp in 1792 who further enlarged the park by exchanging land near Sutton with Ladywood. The Prince of Wales (later Edward VII) attended the Royal Agricultural Show held in the grounds in June 1898 and visited again in 1901. The house, shown *c.*1870, was demolished by 1908.

131 Hartopp Road was named after the family. Sir John Hartopp sold the Four Oaks Estate to a racecourse company in the 1870s. In spite of large investment the racecourse was not successful and was sold to the Marquis of Clanrikarde in 1898 and developed as a residential area with new roads such as Hartopp, Luttrell and Bracebridge. Various covenants prohibited activities such as business use or sale of liquor in order to create a select environment.

132 Elford Cottage, shown in 1907, is typical of the type of housing development in Four Oaks. Many of the houses were built in the 'Arts and Crafts' style with examples by architects such as W.S. Lethaby, C.E. Bateman and W.H. Bidlake.

FOUR OAKS
WESLEYAN CHURCH AND
SCHOOLS.

133 Methodist worship began at Four Oaks before 1800 when a small congregation met at Hill Hook. A later chapel in 'Bell Well Lane' became too small for the increasing population after the railway arrived. A plot of land was given for a new church at the corner of Four Oaks Road and Lichfield Road and the foundation stone was laid in 1902.

134 There were three stages of development as funds allowed—first the nave, completed in 1903 at a cost of £4,200, then the transepts and finally the tower, chancel, choir vestry, schools and church parlour (costing almost £6,000). The architects were Crouch & Butler and the builders James Smith & Sons. The church was built of Weldon stone from Northamptonshire and shows the influence of the Arts & Crafts movement. The opening service was conducted by Rev. Luke Wiseman in 1910 and the church was enlarged in 1969.

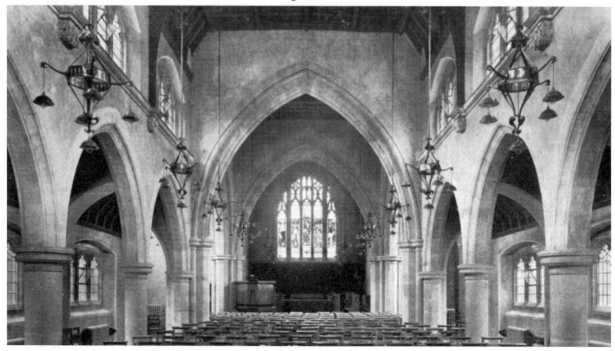

135   Four Oaks Common post office.

136 The Hollies was a large house situated opposite the Park in Four Oaks Road. The building dated from at least 1868, when its then owner, Richard Dorsett, was mentioned in a law dispute. It opened as a VAD hospital in October 1917, closing in April 1919. A wounded soldier can be seen in the garden in this photograph.

137 A group of patients and staff (with assorted pets) are shown here. At least 359 patients were treated including several Canadians, Americans and Australians and two prisoners of war.

138 Photographs survive showing patients receiving treatment at The Hollies.

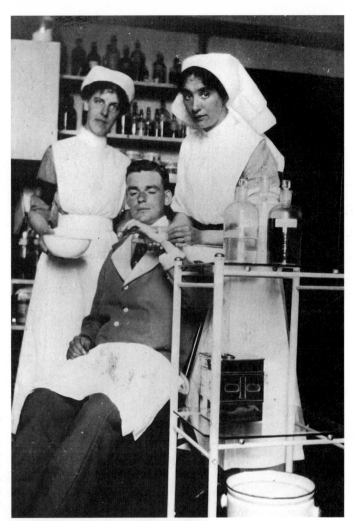

139 A variety of wounds and illnesses were dealt with including gun shot wounds, amputations, shrapnel wounds, gassing, septicaemia, malaria, influenza, gastritis, and many who were described as 'sick'. There was one case of appendicitis and one of varicose veins. Letters survive from grateful patients sometimes reporting their progress and in one case describing less caring treatment endured at another hospital.

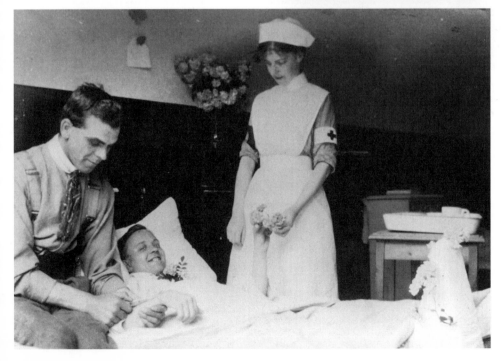

140 Miss Beatrice Cooper was appointed Sister-in-Charge at The Hollies, opened as an extension to Allerton VAD hospital. The Commandant was Beryl Ryland from Moxhull Hall and the Medical Officer in charge was Dr. G.P. Jerome. Miss Cooper was apparently a photographer and kept a record of patients at fancy dress parties, tea parties, concerts and picnics.

141 Five Ways Mere Green is shown *c.*1925. First shown on Greenwood's map of 1821 as 'Mare Green', this was part of the district of Hill in 1853 when it was created a separate ecclesiastical parish with a church dedicated to All Saints. The parish of Four Oaks was formed from this in 1920. Mere Green was the destination for the first bus service from Chester Road in the 1920s.

142 Bishop Vesey built 51 stone houses in Sutton parish including this cottage at Little Sutton, shown in 1956. The houses varied in size but were built to a similar design, using roughly squared stones for most of the walls with quoining at the corners and properly cut stones around doors and windows and a spiral staircase to the upper floor.

143 Houses in Whitehouse Common Road, shown in the 1930s. There was a sufficient population in Whitehouse Common by 1880 for church services to be held at a barn. A mission church opened in 1920 which led to the building of St Chad's Church in Hollyfield Road in 1927 and a new parish was created in 1959.

Little Aston and Streetly

Little Aston is first mentioned in the 13th century. Strictly speaking it is not part of Sutton Coldfield but the area was described as the 'colefield' and it is located on the boundary of Sutton Park and adjacent to Four Oaks. Although there had been some earlier industrial activity in Ford Lane, Little Aston was still largely a rural area in the late 19th century. Maps show a small settlement centred on the junction of Forge Lane and Aldridge Lane with a population of under two hundred. Twentieth-century development has resulted in a community of around three thousand.

Streetly, like Little Aston, is situated in Staffordshire but has close links with Sutton and its Park. Its name is said to derive from the Roman road Ryknield Street which crosses Sutton Park and emerges near the site of the former railway station. It once marked the boundary between Staffordshire and Warwickshire. Much suburban development has taken place this century.

144 The earliest references to Little Aston Hall date from the 13th century. The present house was built around 1730 for Richard Scott from Great Barr Hall. This house was built near the site of the original 13th-century dwelling and is shown *c.*1947.

145 The new house (shown *c.*1910) was restyled by the architect James Wyatt for a later owner, William Tennant, who also commissioned the architect Edward Payne to 'beautify' the hall. The 1730 house was encased in Hollington stone from Uttoxeter and two wings were added to create an Italianate palazzo. Subsequent owners included Edward Parker Jervis (who paid £35,000 for the hall in 1857) and Harry Scribbans who purchased it in 1928 and modernised it. The hall is now converted into apartments and Little Aston Hospital has been built on land formerly part of the park and was officially opened by Princess Anne in 1985.

146 St Peter's Church (shown *c.*1920) at Little Aston was consecrated in 1874. The architect was George Edward Street and it was built on land donated by Edward Parker Jervis at his own expense.

147 The crossroads at Little Aston with the Lodge to the Hall is shown *c.*1920.

148 Streetly station (shown *c.*1920) was located on the railway line linking Walsall with Castle Bromwich and was constructed by the Wolverhampton, Walsall & Midland Junction Railway (which later became the Midland Railway) in 1872. Leaving Streetly, the line runs through Sutton Park where there was once a station and another was situated in Sutton town. There was a further station at Penns near Walmley. All these stations have now closed.

149 Thornhill Road and the Park entrance are shown *c.*1920.

150 Some of the shops in Streetly Village are shown *c.*1920.

151 All Saints' Church, Streetly (shown in 1910) began life as a Mission Church in the parish of Great Barr. The church is situated at the corner of Featherston Road and Foley Road East and the foundation stone was laid on 5 December 1908. The church was licensed for weddings in 1911, and became a separate parish in 1918. In 1908 the building consisted of a nave and chancel.

152 All Saints' after 1920. The war memorial features a life-size figure of Christ and was sculpted from Portland stone by T. Newburn Crook. Complaints from residents forced removal from its original position. In 1954 a large extension was added forming a new nave, chancel and sanctuary, with the original building becoming the south aisle and lady chapel. A further extension in 1975 created a new hall, kitchen and office and a new vicarage was also built.

Banners Gate and New Oscott

The western part of the parish of Sutton was sparsely populated for centuries and was, for the most part, open heath land, which was described as having been 'dreary and desolate' in 1855. Travellers using the Chester Road were often preyed upon by cut-throats, footpads and highwaymen. By the 18th century the situation was particularly bad with many reported crimes, such as the murder of a London silk dyer called John Johnson in March 1729. A local man called Edward Allport was found guilty of Mr. Johnson's murder and was hung and gibbeted at New Oscott, and the area became known as Gibbet Hill. By the 19th century most of the area was farmland and there were several farms such as College Farm. The name 'New Oscott' derives from the Roman Catholic College originally sited at Oscott or Maryvale, Kingstanding (which became known as 'Old Oscott'). Much housing development has taken place in the area around Banners Gate and New Oscott in this century, especially since 1945. Shops were built at the *Beggar's Bush* and at the junction of College Road and Chester Road. New churches were built for the increasing population. Large supermarkets have been built at the corner of Jockey Road and Chester Road in the last 15 years, augmenting the earlier shops.

153 A print dated 1829, drawn by P. Dewint and engraved by W. Radclyffe, shows the view towards Birmingham from the heathland covered in gorse bordering Sutton Park. A lone horseman can be seen on the road, so dangerous in the 18th century that travellers were often armed. Joseph Webster of Penns Hall carried a brace of pistols and a sword.

154 The foundation stone of St Columba's Church (shown 1997) was laid on 28 February 1959 by the mayor of Sutton, Alderman Mrs. M.L. Grounds. The new church was consecrated on 22 October 1960 by the Bishop of Aston, Rt. Rev. Michael Parker. The architect was N.F. Cachemaille-Day and it was built by T. Elvins & Sons Ltd. (the firm which built St Peter's, Maney, more than fifty years earlier). The church and its fittings cost almost £85,000.

155 Princess Alice Orphanage (named after a daughter of Queen Victoria) was founded in 1884 in connection with the Children's Home in London. Architect J.L. Ball from Birmingham designed a grand plan which was gradually completed. The main block (shown here) had various uses such as dining room, chapel and school room.

156 Twelve houses were planned for the Orphanage around a 'village green', with a stable, cow house, piggery, fowl house, barn and dairy beyond the main block. The Misses James from Leamington gave a hospital and 'Copley House' for girls. 'Shaftesbury House' also housed girls, while 'Marsh Memorial House' and 'Seymour House' (shown here with 'Meriden House') housed boys. Two hundred and fifty children were accommodated by 1908. A Tesco supermarket now occupies most of the site.

157 The *Beggar's Bush*, 1997. The original inn took its name (marked on Greenwood's map in 1821) from a small, ancient thorn tree which was cut down in the 1930s for road widening. Local tradition states that a beggar died underneath the bush, which marked the parish boundary and resulted in a dispute over payment for the funeral. However, the English Place Name Society records 'beggar's bush' as a term of reproach for a poor dwelling or soil.

158 Fernwood Grange (shown in 1917) was situated on 8½ acres in Chester Road, opposite Oscott College. It was built for Mr. Alfred Antrobus, a Birmingham jeweller, around 1872. Mr. Antrobus died in 1907 and the estate was purchased by Edward Beston who enlarged the house considerably. It was demolished in 1937 for a housing development but the lodge remains.

159 In 1837 the present Oscott College replaced the original college, founded at Maryvale in 1794 as a school for Roman Catholic boys. The architect was Joseph Potter from Lichfield but Augustus Pugin took over towards the end of construction and added many of his own details. The new college (shown *c*.1910) became the intellectual centre for the English Catholic renewal in the 19th century, and the favourite school of the aristocracy. From 1889 the college ceased to offer secular education, concentrating on its role in training Catholic priests.

160 Bernard Ullathorne, shown in 1889, became the first Roman Catholic Bishop of Birmingham in 1850 and assumed responsibility for Oscott College. He appointed a new president, Dr. John Moore, but inherited serious financial problems resulting from earlier mismanagement, culminating in temporary imprisonment for Ullathorne and Moore on bankruptcy charges. Ullathorne retired in 1888 after 40 years in office and was created an Archbishop. He spent his short retirement at Oscott, dying there in 1889.

Boldmere and Wylde Green

The name Boldmere seems to derive from a marshy pool at the Chester Road end of Boldmere Road. Much of the area was formerly part of the 'Colfield'. Wylde Green probably denotes a 'wild' or sparsely populated area although it is shown as 'Windley Green' on Yates' map of 1789. By 1856 Boldmere was mainly farmland with farmhouses such as Stonehouse Farm (on the corner of Stonehouse and Corbridge Roads) and Booths Farm (at the corner of Darnick and Halton Roads). Much of Boldmere was developed in the Edwardian period although a school was opened in Boldmere Road in 1848. A Roman Catholic chapel, dedicated to St Nicholas, opened in 1840 at the corner of Jockey Road and Boldmere Road (the site is now part of the *Sutton Park Hotel*). The chapel was demolished in 1961 and the new church was built adjacent to the *Park Hotel*. Several shops were built in Boldmere Road. Wylde Green began to develop in the 19th century and both areas were affected by the arrival of the railway with a station in Station Road, Wylde Green, which brought commuters from Birmingham. The population expanded rapidly—for example, in 1901 the population of Boldmere ward was 3,275 and Wylde Green was 1,839, increasing in 1911 to 5,094 and 2,829 respectively. This rapid expansion put great pressure on public services in the area. For example the Health and Highway Department report of 1890 called Boldmere the 'blackspot of the Borough', in particular mentioning the poor state of the roads and the problems of waste water and sewage disposal. Highbridge Road was described as being 'covered with organic filth'. The sculptor Benjamin Creswick (pupil of John Ruskin) lived on Jockey Road. His statue of a man teaching a boy to swim can be seen at Wyndely Swimming Baths (this was originally sited near Powells Pool as a war memorial to members of Boldmere Swimming Club killed during the Second World War).

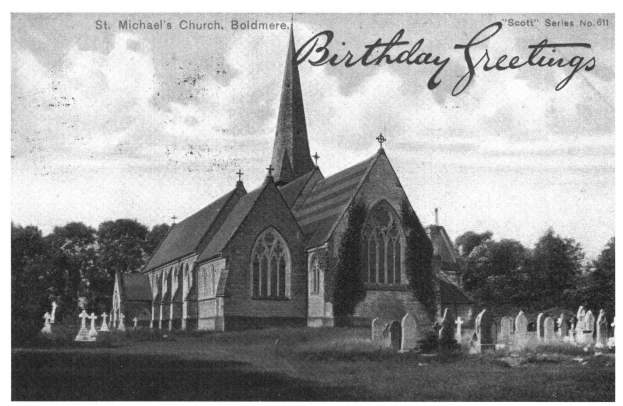

St. Michael's Church. Boldmere.

"Scott" Series No. 611

Birthday Greetings

161 From 1848 services were held in the new school in Boldmere Road. St Michael's Church was designed by J.F. Wedmore and consecrated in 1857. It became a separate ecclesiastical parish on 4 March 1858. Following an increase in population the church was enlarged in 1871 and the spire was added at the same time. The building is shown in 1911. St Michael's was badly damaged by fire in 1964 and partially rebuilt in a modern style.

162 Jockey Road (shown *c.*1921) runs through Boldmere and Wylde Green linking the Chester Road and the Birmingham Road. Mostly developed in this century, only 11 houses were shown on an Ordnance Survey map of 1903 between Birmingham Road and the *Park Hotel,* together with all the dwellings from the Park to College Road (south side).

JOCKEY RD. WYLDE GREEN.

163 A new Congregational Church was opened on 19 June 1898 at the corner of Britwell Road and Highbridge Road to cater for the needs of the growing population. An iron church, it accommodated 200 people and this drawing dates from *c.*1898. It was fitted with wooden benches and cased in pitchpine. The present building is known as Wylde Green United Reformed Church.

164 Wylde Green developed first along the Birmingham Road (shown *c.*1930) which links Chester Road and Sutton. The road was turnpiked in 1827.

165 Large, handsome houses such as Herman House, shown in 1912, were built along its length. Herman House is recorded on the 2nd edition of the 6 in. to one mile OS map, dated 1903. Wylde Green House was another imposing house which occupied a plot of land near the junction of Birmingham Road and Wylde Green Road.

166 Emmanuel Church, Wylde Green (shown 1997) was built as a chapel of ease to St Michael's, Boldmere in 1909-10, and was constructed of red brick. The architect was W.H. Bidlake. A separate parish was created in 1923 and the church was considerably enlarged in 1927 at a cost of £8,000.

167 Penns Lane leads from Wylde Green to Walmley and probably takes its name from Penns at Walmley which was famous for its wire drawing mills. It was the scene of Mary Ashford's death in 1817.

168 A nursing home is shown in Penns Lane, *c.*1900.

Postscript

169 A view looking south along the Parade in the early 1960s with the original Baptist Church on the left (now the site of a McDonald's burger restaurant). The *Museum* public house is on the right.

170 Looking south along the Parade from the junction with the Lower Parade, early 1960s.

171 A view from the early 1960s looking north to the junction of the Parade and Lower Parade, with the parish church in the distance. An interesting comparison can be made with photographs 26 and 27 (which show similar views around 1900) and with the following photograph looking north to the Parade and Lower Parade.

172 A similar view looking north along the Parade in 1997. The Lower Parade and the view towards the parish church are still recognisable but the Parade itself has been considerably changed. The 19th-century shop buildings have been replaced with new shopping developments and the Parade is a pedestrian area.

173 In 1963 the 94-year lease on the land along the Parade expired and the existing shops were eventually demolished and replaced with modern shopping developments. The Gracechurch Centre (shown in 1997), situated on the west side of the Parade, and the Sainsbury Centre (which incorporates the public library) on the east were officially opened in 1974.

174 The Gracechurch Centre (shown 1997) took its name from the location of the head offices of the United Kingdom Provident Institution, owners of the freehold from 1944 who made the development. A ceramic mural shows Sutton Park and Bishop Vesey and allusions to the game of chess (in Bishop's Court, Castle Court and so on) commemorate the internationally known chess player B.H. Wood who lived in Sutton from 1936, while punning on the use of 'bishop' in the depiction of a large chess piece.

175 The United Reformed Church (originally built as the Congregational Church) survived the town centre redevelopment, although its church hall in Station Street was demolished and replaced with a new church centre. This photograph was taken in 1979 after the demolition of Station Street and Park Road and shows the old Council House and the railway station (now surrounded by car parks) in the distance.

176 Further redevelopment has taken place in the South Parade in the 1990s and this photograph shows some of the new shops in the pedestrianised area.

Bibliography

Bassett, John, *Cross City Connections* (1990)

Baxter, Marian, *Sutton Coldfield*, Old Photographs series (1994)

Bedford, W.K. Riland, *History of Sutton Coldfield* (1891)

Beresford, M.W., 'The Economic Individualism of Sutton Coldfield', *Birmingham & Warwickshire Archaeological Society Transactions* (1946)

Birmingham & Warwickshire Archaeological Society, *Sutton Survey*, Interim Reports 1 and 2 1995-6

Birmingham Faces and Places (1889)

Bracken, Agnes, *History of the Forest and Chase of Sutton Coldfield* (1860)

Champ, Judith, *Oscott*, Archdiocese of Birmingham Historical

Chatwin, P.B. and Hartcourt, E.G., 'The Bishop Vesey Houses '..., *Birmingham & Warwickshire Archaeological Society Transactions* (1946)

Commission Publication No.3 (1987)

Congregational Church Manual (various years)

Dictionary of National Biography

Dugdale, W., *Antiquities of Warwickshire* (1656 and 1754)

Gentleman's Magazine (1762, 1801, 1807 and 1844)

History of Sutton by an Impartial Hand (1762)

The Hollies (unpublished album of photographs plus MS notes, *c*.1915-19)

Horsfall, John, *The Iron Masters of Penns* (1971)

Jones, Douglas, *Royal Town of Sutton Coldfield* (3rd edition, 1984)

Jones, Douglas, *Sutton Park* (1982)

Kelly's Directory of Warwickshire (various editions)

Lea, Roger (ed.), *Scenes from Sutton's Past ...* (1989)

Lea, Roger, *Steaming up to Sutton* (1984)

Midgeley, W., *A Short History of the Town and Chase of Sutton Coldfield* (1904)

Minworth School 80th Anniversary 1902-1982

Peers, A., *History and Guide ... of Sutton Coldfield* (1869)

Privett, B.J., *The History of the Parish of St Columba, Sutton Coldfield* (1981)

St Peter's, Maney: 75th Anniversary 1905-80 (1980)

Smith, Francis, *Warwickshire Delineated* (*c*.1820)

Smith, William, *A New ... History of the County of Warwick* (1829)

Sutton Official Guide (1907)

Sutton Park (1980)

Tidmarsh, J.G., *The Sutton Coldfield 15" Gauge Railway* (1990)

Victoria History of the County of Warwick, vol.4 (1947)

Who was Who (1910-9)

Williams, K.J., *A History of Boldmere* (1994)

Williams, K.J., *A History of New Oscott* (1995)

World Scout Jubilee Jamboree (1957)

Index

Roman numbers refer to pages of text, arabic numbers refer to captions.